SMIDGEN OF DREAMS

A FLORILEGIUM OF SCRIBBLED REVERIES.

ASMITA PARIDA

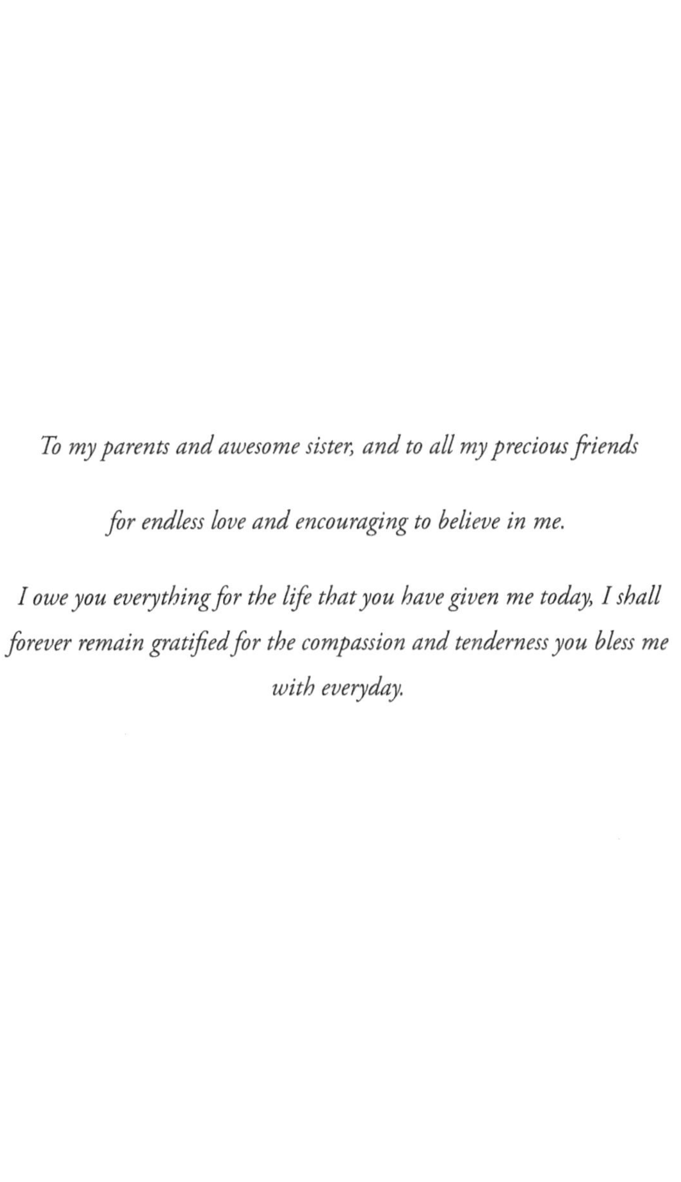

To my parents and awesome sister, and to all my precious friends

for endless love and encouraging to believe in me.

I owe you everything for the life that you have given me today, I shall forever remain gratified for the compassion and tenderness you bless me with everyday.

Contents

Foreword — vii

Preface — ix

Acknowledgements — xi

Prologue — xiii

1. Chapter One — 1
2. ~ — 2
3. Chapter Two — 3
4. ~ — 4
5. Chapter Three — 5
6. ~ — 6
7. Chapter Four — 7
8. ~ — 8
9. Chapter Five — 9
10. ~ — 10
11. Chapter Six — 11
12. ~ — 12
13. Chapter Seven — 13
14. ~ — 14
15. Chapter Eight — 15
16. ~ — 16
17. Chapter Nine — 17
18. ~ — 18
19. Chapter Ten — 19
20. ~ — 20

Contents

21. Chapter Eleven   21

22. ~   22

23. Chapter Twelve   23

24. ~   24

25. Chapter Thirteen   25

26. ~   26

27. Chapter Fourteen   27

28. ~   28

29. Chapter Fifteen   29

30. ~   30

31.   31

32. ~   32

33.   33

34. ~   34

Notes   35

~   37

Foreword

"'When the reality is harsh on you, you start living in dreams.'"

And after a long day of fight, she realized that it was completely useless to fight with me. Moreover, we both could not sleep that night, but at 4 a.m I recieved a text from her and here's what she wrote:

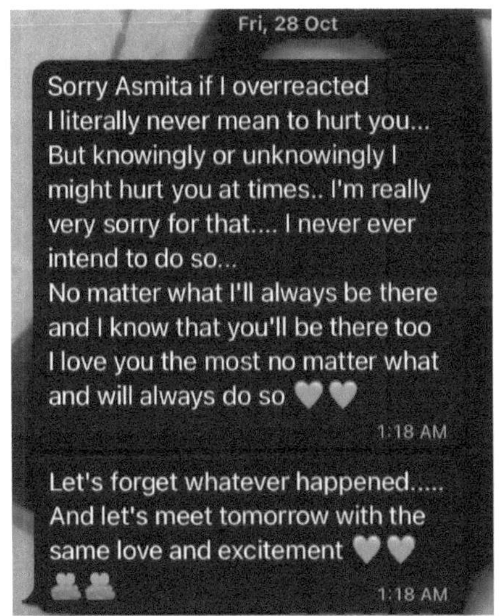

Also, to mention her name, she's *Sheenu Mishra.* A true best friend who not only inspired me to write this book but also helps me everyday to become a better version of myself.

Preface

"When emotions lay bare, unheralded, sheathed in the most fortuitous way, ready to betray the rumination and ultimately leave you flabbergasted."

Our vehemences can be peculiarly soothing, yet could turn out to be pernicious. What matters in the long run, is the way you embrace it; These abhorrent emotions mixed with a tinge of happiness and surreal memories are just the vulnerable phases of your life.

The collection of writings in the book is truly inspired from the idea of learning and knowing the best version of yourself when you are in a circumambient amidst the darkness looking for that smallest light that is nothing but a gleam of hope. Remember, your life is a mosiac of fictional and non-fictional thoughts and all you do is question yourself, "What if it was just a dream?" It is all about enclasping those "smidgen of dreams" and being yourself, thriving to seize the most out of every possible thing even if you're broken. These shattered pieces of you are going to blend into an beautiful ornament of your aura and every ounce of your unheard emotions is going to transmorgify into a delicate rhythm tuning into the song of the universe, stringing to every pygmy chord of tranquility.

...

Acknowledgements

"To the songs, the singers and the movies that galvanized

my emotions and actuated me to pen down my words

together,

To the people I've known and the strangers too, who

joined my roller coaster of spirits and giving me space for

who I am today,

THANKYOU!"

Prologue

"You should put your emotions into words and start writing again", she said. As we sipped our daily cup of tea, talking about how tiring the norms of the world can be. Ohh! to mention her, she is my best friend who would attract alot of attention. Not because of the fact that she had the most beautiful eyes as I would not describe as deep as an ocean but the enchanting sight of the setting sun. She was lively, filled with energy that would filter all your rancor. I, being an overly sensitive personality would not have any recollection of my actions and she in the very moment would bring me back into her vivid world with her eloquent words.

She, was my *wee of impetus and conceit.* Upon days after over deliberation and diffidence, I chose to pen down whatever I could grasp; I would still look for her on the days that I am anxious and she would fabricate my nightmares into a chronology of dreams that I still schlep within my soul everyday.

The unblemished array of memories with her is present in every alphabet that I have scribbled unequivocally in this book; She shall always be my *poetry* that I would keep treasured like the *desicatted rose in the lover's memior.*

...

1. Chapter ONE

For the waves that hauled us closer,
seemed to be in cahoots with destiny.
For the zephyr that whispered serenely,
seemed to have filched your voice with them.
For the twilight that endorsed your simper,
seemed to have a glimpse of the ecstasy of light at the end of the
tunnel.
But, your presence was a sojourn,
all I could incarcerate you reminisce in pieces.
I shall pause here
until you holler my name again.

2. ~

3. Chapter TWO

"We keep this love in a photograph
We made these memories for ourselves
Where our eyes are never closing
Hearts are never broken
And time's forever frozen, still...
~ Ed Sheeran"

As I encapsulated those souvenirs in a frame,
maybe it's a little tattered and torn at the ends
I catechize myself again and again,
How could you be here when you decided to wane away?
I do put you on a pedestal clandestinely,
only in the hope to deliquesce those frozen jiffs.

4. ~

5. Chapter THREE

"Why would you ever kiss me?
I'm not even half as pretty
You gave her your sweater, it's just polyester
But you like her better
Wish I were Heather...
~ Conan Grey"

In the quest of answers, I have embarked on canvassing you
all my contemplation, word by word exists in poetry for you
leaving no crevasse for my elusiveness.
Are you still going to espouse her over me?
Or shall I live in the name of endearment which will immure
me in forged donjon,
so that you can occlude all the presentments above and beyond.

7. Chapter FOUR

"Wise men say
Only fools rush in
But I can't help falling in love with you
Shall I stay?
Would it be a sin
If I can't help falling in love with you?
~ Elvis Presley"

For the first time, my hands tottered as they held yours,
For the first, my voice quivered as I called your name,
a wave of your breath flushed my cheeks
Your eyes reciprocated much more than cues,
while mine were astrayed in yours
Was this love or or just a glimpse of my bovine stupor?
However, living intransigent was streets ahead than
endeavouring to know.

8. ~

9. Chapter FIVE

"And I've heard of a love that comes once in a lifetime
And I'm pretty sure that you are that love of mine
'Cause I'm in a field of dandelions
Wishing on every one that you'll be mine...
~ Ruth B."

Admist the sumptuous bawn of dandelions,
even the winds awed by phantoms about you,
neither I was ascertain about my extant
nor did I want to flare up the verisimilitude,
sundry with golden dreams
ardous with seeking your presence,
I reigned over the ether, the seirras and the aureate dandelions.

11. Chapter SIX

The clangour of woes that asphyxiates my voice,
the time that derides every minute of my agony
I don't know anything except to condone alone.
I beseeched tranquillity and calmness,
but it was all shunned.
In the murk, I set my heart on retreating,
I was, I will exclude into stillness and stillness.

12. ~

13. Chapter SEVEN

"I had all and then most of you
Some and now none of you
Take me back to the night we met
I don't know what I'm supposed to do
Haunted by the ghost of you
Take me back to the night we met...
~ Lord Huron."

A scrape of my heart, I left with you
with each breath, I enunciated your name,
oblivious of chaos
the laughter and cries are now thwarted
I have defrauded my own self
nothing left to live with,
but just a scarce of breaths.

14. ~

15. Chapter EIGHT

They did apprise me not to make abode out of people,
now it left a wound while they are distant.
the heart is now an empty space,
with sprinkling bits of my own self
the setting sun reminded of us
now in the stars, I look for you.
All I could realize was it was unfeasible to reach you,
I miss you and I will miss you.

16. ~

17. Chapter NINE

We delineated the golden hour,
living in the surreal dream
the stars are nothing but us,
we felt loved in our own faults.
We enkindled our little infinity,
between all the odds, you were the even.
maybe you could have lived a little longer?
we'll meet again and I promise you nothing but forever
okay? okay.

18. ~

19. Chapter TEN

"And loving is hard, it don't always work
You just try your best not to get hurt
I used to be mad but now I know
Sometimes it's better to let someone go
It just hadn't hit me yet
The older I get...
~ Sasha Alex Sloan."

And I do miss him,
after days of craving and holding back
with every echo of heart,
maybe I decided to let him go
it was uncanny
was it just me who loved you?
perhaps a goodbye was the only answer.
All I could say was "I guess it was never meant to be"
and set you free.

20. ~

21. Chapter ELEVEN

As I lay down beholding your eyes,

I still do relish the forehead kiss you gave me

your warm breath lights up my heart,

like millions of fireflies that trouce the darkness.

Fingers that interweaved our souls together,

embracing every touch that I've ever dreamt of.

For the first time, the world felt right

and all I coveted was nothing but perpetuity.

22. ~

23. Chapter TWELVE

"Underneath it all I'm held captive by the hole inside
I've been holding back for the fear that you might change
your mind
I'm ready to forgive you, but forgettin' is a harder fight
Little do you know
I need a little more time...
- Alex and sierra."

The eternal dusks
in the dwam, I lay
evoked in thoughts about you,
no, he wasn't justifiable
in the depths of haunted memories
sinking in the tears, my shadows left behind
I incarcerated myself,
and somewhere between "forgetting and forgiving"
I unshackled my tangled beats of my heart.

24. ~

25. Chapter THIRTEEN

The crumbling skin,
garnered from the ashes
maybe every end had a new story to begin,
hoping to suffuse even tiniest cranny of darkness
the walls might fall again and again,
remember to extricate yourself
from those strangles of squalid rope,
it is nothing but to hark back to eensy hope.

26. ~

27. Chapter FOURTEEN

"Oh, I hope you're happy
But not like how you were with me
I'm selfish, I know, I can't let you go
So find someone great, but don't find no one better
I hope you're happy, but don't be happier...
Olivia Rodrigo."

I begrudge the wind,

that caress your aura in my absence

I am discontented when the rain

that touches you the way I did,

in the quandary, my selfishness tore us apart

you love her now and it's okay,

and, in this awaiting

my mind envisaged us together

but, I was left behind long ago.

28. ~

29. Chapter FIFTEEN

"Someone give me some paper
Someone give me some crayons
I'm feeling like a child
I need something to play on
I'm trying hard to trust you
When you say give me your hand
Baby, I'm falling
I hope you catch me when I land...
~ Kat Dahlia."

And eyes were inquisitive about you,
and they say "home is a person"
but you were my secret to paradise,
I wrote when I missed you
but, I'll never share you even with my own words,
the butterflies in my stomach
could not have been more happier,
swirl me around while I blush
I will ask nothing more,
but a promise to keep me close.

31. .....

"She's a fallen angel, who isn't a secret anymore. Victim of anxiety, heartbreaks and those cruel nightmares, she decides not to melt herself into hell anymore. Those shattered pieces of memories and betrayal from footprints that she followed, pierced her skin and every ounce of blood she lost gave her a chance to leave her fears"

~ AND IT'S OKAY TO NOT BE OKAY.

32. ~

33. .....

" The sky flushed in red, the moon that lit his face and the warmth of his touch, brought my lost pieces of love to live again. yes, maybe he loves me more but I don't know. And on the darkest of days, he picked me when I was bruised with pain and painted a red hue. I would have destroyed myself in a million ways but he held my hand and now I know I am at a better place. And in the end, it is about us, about love we had and I am stuck here with those broken glimpses. We'll meet again, till then, I keep my fingers crossed and goodbye my love.

~ SHE , WHO IS TOO AFRAID TO LET YOU GO.

34. ~

Notes